LOSE WEIGHT FOR GOOD

SLOW COOKER DIET FOR BEGINNERS

CookNation

LOSE WEIGHT FOR GOOD: SLOW COOKER DIET FOR BEGINNERS

Disclaimer

CONTENTS

SNACKS   91

CONVERSION CHART   95

INTRODUCTION

Inexpensive, healthy meals for you and your family with the minimum of fuss

Welcome to Lose Weight For Good: Slow Cooker Diet For Beginners. This collection of easy to prepare and delicious low-calorie recipes will help you make inexpensive, healthy meals for you and your family with the minimum of fuss. During the colder months our bodies naturally crave warm, filling and comforting food which can often result in overeating, weight gain and sluggishness.

These delicious recipes use simple and inexpensive fresh ingredient; are packed full of flavour and goodness, and show that you can enjoy maximum taste with minimum calories. Each recipe has been tried, tested, and enjoyed time and time again. With so many delicious recipes to choose from we're sure you'll agree that diet can still mean delicious.

PREPARATION

All of the recipes take no longer than 10-15 minutes to prepare. Browning the meat will make a difference to the taste of your recipe but if you really don't have the time, don't worry. It will still taste good.

There are a number of 'shortcut' ingredients like salsa and taco rub throughout the book, but there is also the option to make these from scratch if you have the time.

All meat and vegetables should be cut into even sized pieces.

Meat generally cooks faster than vegetables, although root vegetables can take longer, so make sure everything is bite-sized.

All meat should be trimmed of visible fat and the skin removed.

NUTRITION

All of the recipes in this collection are balanced low fat family meals under 500 calories which should keep you feeling full and help you avoid snacking in-between meals. All recipes have serving suggestions; the calories noted are per serving of the recipe ingredients only, so bear that in mind.

LOW COST

Slow cooking is ideal for cheaper meat cuts. The 'tougher' cuts used in this collection of recipes are transformed into meat which melts-in-your-mouth and helps to keep the costs down. We've also made sure not to include too many one-off ingredients which are used for a single recipe and never used again. All the herbs and spices listed can be used in multiple recipes throughout the book.

USING YOUR SLOW COOKER: A FEW THINGS

All cooking times are a guide. Make sure you get to know your own slow cooker so that you can adjust timings accordingly.

A spray of one cal cooking oil in the cooker before adding ingredients will help with cleaning or you can buy liners.

Be confident with your cooking. Feel free to use substitutes to suit your own taste and don't let a missing herb or spice stop you making a meal - you'll almost always be able to find something to replace it.

ABOUT COOKNATION

CookNation is the leading publisher of innovative and practical recipe books for the modern, health conscious cook.

CookNation titles bring together delicious, easy and practical recipes with their unique no nonsense approach - making cooking for diets and healthy eating fast, simple and fun.

With a range of #1 best-selling titles - from the innovative 'Skinny' calorie-counted series, to the 5:2 Diet Recipes collection - CookNation recipe books prove that 'Diet' can still mean 'Delicious'!

To browse all CookNation's recipe books visit www.bellmackenzie.com

 **CookNation**

LOSE WEIGHT FOR GOOD

SLOW COOKER DIET FOR BEGINNERS

SLOW COOKER CHICKEN DISHES

· ·

RUSTIC CHICKEN STEW

480 calories per serving

Ingredients

- 2kg/4½ lb skinless chicken pieces
- 2 tbsp plain/all purpose flour
- 1 onion, chopped
- 1 red (bell) pepper, sliced
- 2 cloves garlic, crushed
- 2 400g/14oz tins chopped tomatoes
- 1 tsp dried rosemary
- 1 handful pitted green olives
- 1 tsp anchovy paste
- 3 bay leaves
- 500ml/2 cups chicken stock
- Low cal cooking spray
- Salt & pepper to taste

Method

1 Season the chicken pieces well. Dust with the flour and then quickly brown in a large pan with a little low cal cooking spray.

2 When browned, remove the chicken from the pan and place in the slow cooker with all the other ingredients. Leave to cook on low for 5-6 hours or high for 3-4 hours with the lid tightly shut or until the chicken is cooked through and tender.

3 If you prefer the sauce to be a little thicker, continue cooking for about 45 min on the high setting with the lid removed.

CHEFS NOTE

Widely known in Italy as 'Hunter's Stew', this hearty meal has kept the faith with countless hunters and gatherers over the years. Regional variations of this dish are common throughout Italy - this rustic version is one of the most popular.

SWEET ASIAN CHICKEN

256 calories per serving

Ingredients

- 500g/1lb 2oz skinless chicken breasts
- 2 garlic cloves, crushed
- 1 onion, chopped
- 60ml/¼ cup honey
- 2 tbsp tomato puree/paste
- 4 tbsp light soy sauce
- 2 carrots cut into batons
- Pinch crushed chilli
- 250ml/1 cup fresh orange juice
- 1 tsp sunflower oil
- 1 tsp cornstarch dissolved in a little water to form a paste

Method

1 Combine all the ingredients in a bowl and add to the slow cooker.

2 Cook on low for 5-6 hours or on high for 3-4 hours with the lid tightly shut or until the chicken is cooked through and tender. Add a little water during cooking if needed.

3 Serve with fine egg noodles or rice. You could add a garnish of spring onions/scallions & sesame seeds.

CHEFS NOTE
The honey, soy and orange juice in this dish make it a hit with the kids and adds a little eastern flavour to evening meal times.

GREEN PESTO CHICKEN THIGHS

469 calories per serving

Ingredients

- 500g/1lb 2oz skinless, boneless chicken thighs
- 175g/6oz green pesto
- 250ml/1 cup buttermilk
- 1 tsp salt
- 50g/2oz asparagus spears
- 2 cloves garlic, crushed
- 1 onion, chopped

Method

1 Smother the chicken thighs in pesto and carefully combine with all the other ingredients, except the asparagus spears, in the slow cooker. Cook on low for 5-6 hours or on high for 3-4 hours with the lid tightly shut.

2 Half an hour before cooking ends add the asparagus spears. Ensure the chicken is cooked through and tender.

3 Serve with fresh green salad and crusty bread.

CHEFS NOTE

Originating from Northern Italy, pesto has been around since Ancient Roman times. It's pounded blend of basil, cheese, pine nuts, salt and olive oil create a distinctive taste which works well with meat. Pour any juices from the bottom of the slow cooker over the chicken before serving.

HONEYED CHICKEN WINGS

453
calories per serving

Ingredients

- 16 large skinless chicken wings
- 1 tsp freshly grated ginger (or ½ tsp ground ginger)
- 2 cloves garlic, crushed
- 1 tbsp runny honey
- 1 tbsp light soy sauce
- 1 tsp sesame oil
- 1 tbsp lemon juice
- 1 carrot peeled into ribbons
- 4 spring onions/scallions chopped
- 120ml/½ cup stock
- 2 tsp sesame seeds
- Salt and pepper to taste

Method

1 Coat the chicken wings in the runny honey and then combine with all the other ingredients, except the spring onions and sesame seeds, in the slow cooker. Leave to cook on high for approx 4 hours or low for 6 hours.

2 Serve sprinkled with the spring onions and sesame seeds.

CHEFS NOTE
This is a lovely sweet tender chicken recipe which is great to share with family & friends.

FALL OFF THE BONE WHOLE SLOW COOKED CHICKEN

446 calories per serving

Ingredients

- 2kg/ 4½lb skinless whole chicken
- 2 onions, sliced into rings
- Dried rub mix of :
- 1 tsp each garlic powder, thyme, paprika & onion powder + pinch salt

Method

1 Combine the dried ingredients together and rub really well into the fresh chicken.

2 Place the onions in the bottom of the slow cooker and put the chicken on top. Cook on low for 7-8 hours with the lid tightly shut. Ensure the chicken is cooked through.

3 Serve with your choice of vegetables, potatoes or salad.

CHEFS NOTE

Whole cooked chicken really comes into it's own in the slow cooker. This super simple recipe will give you the heart of a meal which, with leftovers, can last a couple of days.

ZINGY LIME CHICKEN

200
calories per serving

Ingredients

- 500g/1lb 2oz skinless chicken breasts
- 3 tbsp lime juice
- Bunch fresh coriander/cilantro chopped and some to garnish
- 1 sliced green chilli (or a pinch of dried chilli flakes)
- 400g/14oz salsa (or make your own)
- 4 tsp taco seasoning (or make your own)

- Salsa: Add 1 onion chopped, 1 clove garlic crushed, 1 green chilli chopped to 2 x 400g/14oz tins chopped tomatoes + sea salt to taste
- Taco Seasong: 2 tsp mild chilli powder, 1 ½ tsp ground cumin, ½ tsp paprika, ¼ tsp each of onion powder, garlic powder, dried oregano & crushed chilli flakes, 1 tsp each of sea salt & black pepper

Method

1 Put everything together in the slow cooker making sure the chicken is covered with the rest of the ingredients. With the lid tightly shut, leave to cook for 4-5 hours on high or 5-6 hours on the low setting.

2 Ensure the chicken is cooked through and tender then shred it a little with 2 forks and serve with a fresh green salad/rice or quesadillas (flour tortilla).

CHEFS NOTE

Packed with protein, skinless chicken breasts are a great low fat meat to use in the slow cooker. The citrus lightness of this recipe is perfect. for summer months as well as a welcome taste bud infusion during the colder seasons.

CHICKEN & ALMONDS

311
calories per serving

Ingredients

- 500g/1lb 2oz skinless chicken breasts, cut into chunks
- 1 tbsp ground almonds
- ½ tsp paprika
- 2 red (bell) peppers, sliced
- 1 onion, chopped
- 2 cloves garlic, crushed
- 1 tbsp white wine vinegar
- 2 tbsp chopped flat leaf parsley
- 1 400g/14oz tin chopped tomatoes
- 300g/11oz tinned haricot beans, drained
- ½ tsp dried chilli flakes
- 100g/3½oz frozen peas
- Low cal cooking spray
- Salt & pepper to taste

Method

1 Brown the chicken pieces in a little low cal spray. Add all the ingredients, except the parsley, into the slow cooker. Season, cover and leave to cook on high for 3-4 hours or low for 5-6 hours.

2 Sprinkle with chopped parsley and serve with rice and/or crusty bread.

CHEFS NOTE
This Spanish inspired dish is great as a main meal but can also be served as a delicious ciabatta topping.

BBQ CHICKEN

210 calories per serving

Ingredients

- 450g/1lb skinless chicken breasts
- 1 tsp each, smoked paprika & garlic powder
- 60ml/¼ cup chicken stock/broth
- ½ tsp each ground cumin & ground coriander/cilantro

- 1 tbsp brown sugar
- 3 tbsp Worcestershire sauce or steak sauce
- ½ tsp salt
- 3 tbsp tomato puree/paste or ketchup

Method

1 Put all the ingredients into the slow cooker. Mix well, cover and leave to cook on low for 4-5 hours or until the chicken is cooked through and tender.

2 Shred the chicken breasts with 2 forks and mix back into the sauce at the bottom of the slow cooker.

3 If the sauce needs to be thickened, continue to cook on high for up to 45 mins with the lid off. Alternatively if it's too sticky, add a little water to loosen up.

4 Serve with salad or in sandwich rolls with mayonnaise and BBQ sauce.

CHEFS NOTE

When the chicken is shredded and mixed back into the sauce, you should be left with a moist versatile mixture which is effectively the poultry version of the BBQ classic 'pulled pork'.

LOVELY LEMONY GARLICKY CHICKEN

208 calories per serving

Ingredients

- 500g/1lb 2oz skinless chicken breasts
- 3 garlic cloves, crushed
- 3 tbsp lemon juice
- 1 onion, chopped
- 1 tsp runny honey
- 1 tsp cornstarch dissolved in a little water to make a paste
- 500ml/2 cups chicken stock/broth
- Salt & pepper to taste
- Bunch fresh basil, chopped

Method

1 Combine all the ingredients in the slow cooker and leave to cook on low for 5-6 hours or on high for 3-4 hours with the lid tightly shut. Ensure the chicken is cooked through and tender.

2 Serve with steamed vegetables and rice to soak up the juices.

CHEFS NOTE
This is a really simple protein-packed dish that really benefits from using fresh basil.

LUSCIOUS ITALIAN CHICKEN

235 calories per serving

Ingredients

- 500g/1lb 2oz skinless chicken breasts
- 2 400g/14oz tins low fat condensed chicken or mushroom soup
- 100g/3½ oz mushrooms, sliced
- 1 onion, chopped
- Salt & pepper to taste

- 1 garlic clove, crushed
- 2 tbsp fat free cream cheese

Dried rub mix of:
- 1 teaspoon each oregano, rosemary & thyme

Method

1 Rub the chicken breasts with the dried herb mix and combine all the ingredients into the slow cooker. Cook on low for 5-6 hours or on high for 3-4 hours with the lid tightly shut.

2 Ensure the chicken is cooked through and tender; serve with vegetables, spaghetti, rice or noodles.

CHEFS NOTE

With a lovely creamy consistency, this Italian inspired dish makes the most of that wonderful 'cheat' ingredient - condensed soup!

PEANUT BUTTER CHICKEN

245 calories per serving

Ingredients

- 500g/1lb 2oz skinless chicken breast, diced
- 1 red (bell) pepper, sliced
- 1 onion, chopped
- 4 tbsp low fat peanut butter
- 2 tbsp lime juice
- 120ml/½ cup chicken stock/broth
- 1 tbsp soy sauce
- 1 tsp each ground cumin & coriander/cilantro
- ½ tsp paprika
- Salt & pepper to taste
- Low cal cooking spray

Method

1 In a frying pan quickly brown the chicken in a little low cal spray.

2 Add all the ingredients to the slow cooker, season, cover and leave to cook on low for 4-5 hours or high for 3-4 hours. Make sure the chicken is cooked through and serve with noodles & beansprouts.

CHEFS NOTE

Peanut butter chicken is delicious. You can really 'lift' the dish by serving with fresh lime wedges.

MUSTARD TARRAGON CHICKEN

312
calories per serving

Ingredients

- 500g/1lb 2oz skinless chicken breasts
- 2 tbsp fresh chopped tarragon
- 1 tsp mild mustard, or more to taste
- 400g/14oz new potatoes
- 500ml/2 cups chicken stock/broth
- 200g/7oz broad beans
- 200g/7oz tenderstem broccoli
- Low cal cooking spray
- Salt & pepper to taste
- 3 tbsp low fat crème fraiche or fat free Greek yoghurt

Method

1 Quickly brown the chicken breast in a little low cal spray and thinly slice the potatoes with their skins still on.

2 Place all the ingredients, except the crème fraiche, in the slow cooker and season well. Cover and leave to cook on high for 2-3 hours or until the chicken is tender and cooked through.

3 Remove the chicken from the slow cooker, stir through the crème fraiche and pour the vegetable sauce over the chicken.

CHEFS NOTE

If you prefer your veg to have some crunch to it, hold off adding to the slow cooker until about 30-45 mins before the end of cooking time.

SIMPLE CHICKEN CURRY

223 calories per serving

Ingredients

- 500g/1lb 2oz skinless chicken breasts
- 1 onion, chopped
- 1 tbsp tomato puree/paste
- 3 cloves garlic, crushed
- 1 tsp low fat butter spread
- 1 tbsp fresh grated ginger (or use 1 tsp of ginger powder)
- 1 tsp garam masala
- 1 tsp ground cumin
- 1 tsp turmeric
- ½ tsp chilli powder
- 250ml/1 cup low fat Greek yoghurt
- 375ml/1 ½ cups passata/sieved tomatoes
- Salt & pepper to taste

Method

1 Combine all the ingredients, except the yoghurt, into the slow cooker. Cook on low for 5-6 hours or on high for 3-4 hours with the lid tightly shut.

2 Ensure the chicken is cooked through and tender, turn off the heat and stir in the yoghurt.

3 Serve with green beans and naan bread.

CHEFS NOTE
The mix of spices suggested in the recipe is preferable but it is fine to substitute with curry powder if you are in a rush or struggling with store cupboard ingredients.

CHIPOTLE CHICKEN

198 calories per serving

Ingredients

- 500g/1lb 2oz skinless chicken breasts
- 1 onion, finely chopped
- 1 red onion, sliced
- 3 garlic cloves, crushed
- ½ tsp brown sugar
- 2 tsp chipotle paste
- 1 400g/14oz tin chopped tomatoes
- 2 tbsp fresh chopped flat leaf parsley
- 2 tsp sunflower oil
- Salt & pepper to taste

Method

1 Gently sauté the onion and garlic in the sunflower oil. Remove and quickly brown the chicken breasts in the same pan.

2 Add all the ingredients, except the red onion and parsley, into the slow cooker. Season, cover and leave to cook on high for 2-3 hours or low for 4-5 hours until the meat is tender and cooked through.

3 Shred the chicken with two forks, mix well and serve with the parsley and raw red onion slices on top. Also good with a dollop of fat free Greek yoghurt on the side.

CHEFS NOTE

Chipotle paste is essentially smokey chilli paste from the Mexican Chipotle chilli. If you have difficulty sourcing, just substitute for regular chillies and a little smoked paprika.

CHICKEN & MUSTARD LEEKS

290 calories per serving

Ingredients

- 500g/1lb 2oz skinless chicken breasts
- 1 tbsp plain/all purpose flour
- 100g/3½oz lean, back bacon
- 2 leeks, chopped
- 2 tbsp Dijon mustard
- 1 tsp mustard powder

- 250ml/1 cup chicken stock/broth
- 200g/7oz potatoes, cut into slices
- 1 bay leaf
- 300g/11oz spinach
- Low cal cooking spray
- Salt & pepper to taste

Method

1 Season the chicken and coat well in the flour. Add a little low cal spray to a frying pan and quickly brown the breasts.

2 Add all the ingredients to the slow cooker, cover, stir well and leave to cook on high for 2-3 hours or low for 4-5 hours.

3 Remove the chicken from the slow cooker, slice into diagonal strips and ladle the spinach & potato mixture over the top – along with as much of the sauce as you prefer. If you need more liquid during cooking add a little more stock.

CHEFS NOTE
The mustard in this recipe should be adjusted to your own taste. You can also use wholegrain mustard if you prefer.

CHICKEN, GARLIC & WINE

211 calories per serving

Ingredients

- 500g/1lb 2oz skinless chicken breasts
- 1 lemon, sliced
- 2 onions, chopped
- 6 garlic cloves, sliced
- 120ml/½ cup dry white wine
- 120ml/½ cup chicken stock/broth
- 150g/5oz French beans
- Salt & pepper to taste

Method

1 Season the chicken. Add a little low cal spray to a frying pan and quickly brown the breasts. Add all the ingredients to the slow cooker. Cover, stir well and leave to cook on high for 2-3 hours or low for 4-5 hours.

2 Serve with crusty bread to mop up the delicious lemon juices. If you need more liquid during cooking add a little more stock.

CHEFS NOTE
If you prefer your beans crunchy you can hold off adding them until about 20 minutes before the end of cooking.

CHICKEN & APRICOTS

225 calories per serving

Ingredients

- 500g/1lb 2oz skinless chicken breasts
- 1 tbsp plain/ all purpose flour
- 2 garlic cloves, crushed
- 1 tbsp freshly grated ginger
- 1 tsp each ground cumin & coriander/ cilantro
- ½ tsp ground cinnamon
- 1 tsp runny honey
- 1 tbsp lemon juice
- 1 400g/14oz tin apricots (in juice)
- ½ cup/120ml chicken stock/broth
- Salt & pepper to taste

Method

1 Mix the flour, cinnamon, cumin & coriander together and combine with the chicken breasts.

2 Add all the other ingredients, except the apricots, but including the apricot juice to the slow cooker. Stir well, cover and leave to cook on high for 2-3 hours or low for 4-5 hours.

3 Add the apricots to the mixture, leave to warm through and serve with steamed greens.

CHEFS NOTE
Adding the apricots towards the end of the cooking time prevents them becoming a pulp and retains their form.

LOSE
WEIGHT
FOR GOOD
SLOW COOKER DIET
FOR BEGINNERS

SLOW COOKER
BEEF DISHES

ITALIAN MEATBALLS

323 calories per serving

Ingredients

- 650g/1lb 7oz lean, minced/ground beef
- 1 slice bread, whizzed into bread crumbs
- ½ onion, finely chopped
- Handful fresh parsley, chopped
- 1 large free range egg
- 1 clove garlic, crushed
- ½ tsp salt
- 2 400g/14 oz tins chopped tomatoes
- 2 tbsp tomato puree/paste
- 250ml/1 cup beef stock/broth
- 1 tsp each dried basil, oregano & thyme

Method

1 Combine together the beef, breadcrumbs, egg, onion, garlic and half the salt. (You can do it with your hands or for super-speed put it all into a food mixer).

2 Once the ingredients are properly mixed together, use your hands to shape into about 20-24 meat balls. Add all the ingredients to the slow cooker and combine well. Cover and leave to cook on low for 5-6 hours or 3-4 hours on high. Ensure the beef is well cooked and serve with spaghetti, parmesan and a green salad.

CHEFS NOTE

Meatballs are easy to make and never a disappointment to eat. The simple sauce accompanying the meat here is lovely as it is, but a dash of Worcestershire sauce or a tsp of marmite will give it additional depth.

BUDAPEST'S BEST BEEF GOULASH

228 calories per serving

Ingredients

- 900g/2lbs lean stewing beef cut into chunks (trim off any fat)
- 1 red (bell) pepper, sliced
- 3 cloves garlic, crushed
- 250ml/1 cup beef stock/broth or water
- 250ml/1 cup red wine
- 1 400g/14oz tin chopped tomatoes
- 1 tbsp tomato puree/paste
- 1 tsp paprika
- 1½ tbsp plain/all purpose flour
- 1 onion, chopped
- Low cal cooking oil
- Salt & pepper to taste

Method

1 Season the beef and quickly brown in a smoking hot pan with a little low cal spray. Remove from the pan and dust with flour (the easiest way is to put the beef and flour into a plastic bag and give it a good shake). Add all the ingredients to the slow cooker and combine well.

2 Leave to cook on low with the lid tightly shut for 5-6 hours or until the beef is tender and cooked through. If you want to thicken up a little, leave to cook for a further 45 mins with the lid off.

3 Lovely with a salad & some crusty bread or serve with sour cream and tagliatelle pasta.

CHEFS NOTE

Goulash is a European dish which suits the slow cooker beautifully. After hours of gentle cooking this 'tougher' meat becomes a tender cut which just melts in the mouth.

GINGER BEEF

338 calories per serving

Ingredients

- 675g/1½lb silverside beef/round steak, cubed
- 2 garlic cloves, crushed
- 370ml/1½ cups beef stock/broth
- 1 red (bell) pepper, sliced
- 4 carrots, sliced
- 1 onion, chopped
- 2 tbsp soy sauce
- 1 tbsp freshly grated ginger
- 1 tbsp cornflour mixed with 3 tbsp water
- 100g/3½oz frozen peas
- Salt & pepper to taste

Method

1 Add all the ingredients, except the peas, to the slow cooker. Season well, cover and leave to cook on low for 5-6 hours or high for 3-4 hours.

2 An hour before the end of cooking, add the peas and continue to cook until both the beef and peas are tender.

CHEFS NOTE
Ginger and beef are a great combination and often used in Chinese cookery. Use low salt soy sauce if you want to be extra healthy.

CHILLI CON CARNE

440
calories per
serving

Ingredients

- 550g/1¼ lb lean, minced/ground beef
- 1 400g/14oz tin chopped tomatoes
- 1 400g/14oz tin kidney beans, drained
- 1 large onion, chopped
- 250ml/1 cup beef stock/broth
- 250ml/1 cup tomato passata/sieved tomatoes

- 1 tsp each of brown sugar, oregano, cumin, chilli powder, paprika & garlic powder
- ½ tsp salt
- Low cal cooking spray

Method

1 Brown the mince and onions in a frying pan. Add all the ingredients into the slow cooker and combine well. Leave to cook on low for 5-6 hours or high for 3-4 hours with the lid tightly closed.

2 Once the meat is fully cooked through, serve with rice or tortilla chips and a dollop of low fat yoghurt or crème fraiche.

CHEFS NOTE

The Spanish name simply means 'chilli with meat' and this dish has been a Tex-Mex classic since before the days of the American frontier settlers. Slow cooking the mince beef really allows the flavour to develop.

ENCHILADA EL SALVADOR

324 calories per serving

Ingredients

- 450g/1lb lean, minced/ground beef
- 1 onion, chopped
- 1 green (bell) pepper, chopped
- 1 400g/14oz tin black beans, drained
- 2 400g/14oz tins chopped tomatoes
- 250ml/1 cup beef stock/broth or boiling water
- ½ tsp chilli powder

- 4 tsp taco seasoning

Or make your own:

- 2 tsp mild chilli powder, 1 ½ tsp ground cumin, ½ tsp paprika, ¼ tsp each of onion powder, garlic powder, dried oregano & crushed chilli flakes, 1 tsp each of sea salt & black pepper

Method

1 Add all the ingredients to the slow cooker and combine well. Leave to cook on low with the lid tightly on for 5-6 hours or 3-4 hours on high, until the beef is tender and cooked through. If you want to thicken it up a little leave, to cook for a further 45 mins with the lid off.

2 Serve with flour tortillas, shredded salad, grated cheese and sour cream (or Greek yoghurt).

CHEFS NOTE

Inspired by the flavours of Tex Mex this dish is great fun to eat as a family with everyone helping themselves across the table making their very own perfect enchilada!

BEST BEEF BRISKET

Ingredients

- 2¼ kg/5 lbs beef brisket trimmed of fat
- 4 large onions, sliced into rounds
- 500ml/2 cups beef stock/broth
- 4 bay leaves
- 3 garlic cloves, peeled
- Salt & pepper to taste

Method

1 Season the brisket generously with salt and pepper and brown quickly in a smoking hot dry pan. Lay the onion slices on the bottom of the slow cooker and add the beef along with the rest of the ingredients.

2 Leave to cook with the lid tightly on for 7-9 hours on low. It's best to turn over half way through cooking but don't worry too much if you can't do that. Ensure the beef is super-tender and cooked through. Leave to rest for 20 minutes before slicing.

CHEFS NOTE
Brisket is another beef cut which really benefits from the slow cooker as it tenderizes slowly and evenly in its own juices without drying it out.

SLOW SCOTTISH STOVIES

333 calories per serving

Ingredients

- 175g/6oz potatoes, diced
- 2 large onions, chopped
- 250ml/1 cup vegetable stock/broth
- 450g/1lb left over roast beef (or other cooked red meat)
- Salt & pepper to taste

Method

1 Combine all the ingredients together in the slow cooker and cook on low for 5-6 hours or high for 3-4 hours with the lid tightly shut. The liquid should all be gone by the end of the cooking time, if it hasn't, remove the lid and leave to cook for a little longer.

2 Stir through and serve in bowls with British brown sauce if you have it!

CHEFS NOTE

This is a great recipe to use up any cooked leftover red meat you might have. Traditionally it's served with plain Scottish oatcakes and it's super-simple to make. You can also used cubed corned beef in this recipe.

RAGU A LA BOLOGNESE

344
calories per serving

Ingredients

- 500g/1lb 2oz lean, minced/ground beef
- 1 400g/14oz tin chopped tomatoes
- 250ml/1 cup passata/sieved tomatoes
- 1 tsp each dried oregano & thyme
- 1 stick celery chopped
- 2 bay leaves

- 1 tbsp tomato puree/paste
- 3 garlic cloves, crushed
- 2 onions, chopped
- Salt and pepper to taste
- Low cal cooking spray

Method

1 Quickly brown the meat in a frying pan with a little low cal spray. Combine all the ingredients in the slow cooker and close the lid tightly.

2 Leave to cook on low for 5-6 hours or high for 3-4 hours.

3 Make sure the meat is cooked through and serve with rigatoni, penne or spaghetti.

CHEFS NOTE

Nothing can be simpler or more satisfying than spaghetti bolognese. You can add mushrooms and peppers to the recipe if you like, plus a dash or two of Worcestershire sauce gives extra depth.

PEPPERS & STEAK

250 calories per serving

Ingredients

- 450g/1lb braising steak/beef chuck
- 120ml/ ½ cup soy sauce
- 2 tsp ground black pepper
- 3 cloves garlic, crushed
- 3 red or green (bell) peppers, sliced
- 2 onions, chopped
- 1 tbsp cornflour
- 250ml/1 cup water

Method

1 Slice the steak and vegetables then add everything to the slow cooker, except the water and cornflour. Season, cover and leave to cook on low for 3-5 hours or until the meat is tender and cooked through. (Add a little water during cooking if the meat becomes too dry).

2 Mix together the cornflour and water into a paste, add to the slow cooker and cook for another 20-30 mins with the lid off or until the sauce is nice and thick.

CHEFS NOTE
By slow cooking for a few hours the braising steak should be transformed into a tender cut which can be served on rice or as the heart of a lovely warm salad.

ALMONDS, BEEF & OLIVES

392 calories per serving

Ingredients

- 600g/1lb 5oz lean stewing steak/chuck steak, cubed
- 250ml/1 cup beef stock/broth
- 60ml/¼ cup red wine
- 1 tsp each smoked paprika, dried basil & rosemary
- 1 tbsp plain/all purpose flour
- 200g/7oz pitted olives
- 25g/1oz chopped almonds
- Salt & pepper to taste

Method

1 Season the beef and coat well in the plain flour. Add all the ingredients, except the olives, to the slow cooker and leave to cook on low for 4-6 hours or until the beef is tender.

2 Add a little more stock or wine during cooking if needed and adjust the seasoning. 20 minutes before the end of cooking add the olives, warm through and serve.

CHEFS NOTE

This dish is delicious served with creamed spinach and/or honeyed carrots. Feel free to use a different mix of dried herbs to suit your taste. You can also add a tablespoon of tomato puree during cooking to thicken if you prefer.

SLOW COOKER
PORK DISHES

··

PERFECT PULLED PORK

280
calories per serving

Ingredients

- 900g/2lb pork butt (shoulder)
- 1 onion, chopped
- 250ml/1 cup BBQ sauce or ketchup
- 250ml/1 cup beef stock/broth or boiling water
- 1 packet BBQ dry rub

Or make your own:
- 1 tbsp each of garlic powder, brown sugar, onion powder,
- celery salt, paprika + 1 tsp each mild chilli powder & cumin

Method

1 Combine all the spices together and cover the pork in the dry spice rub. Add the stock, onion & BBQ sauce and then place the pork on top. Leave to cook on high for 6-8 hours with the lid tightly closed. Ideally you should turn the pork over half way through cooking, but if you can't do that don't worry.

2 Once the pork is tender remove it from the slow cooker. Leave to rest for as long as you can resist and then use your hands or 2 forks to pull the pork apart.

3 Once it's all shredded, place in a bowl and remove the cooking liquid from the slow cooker. Pour the liquid onto the pork to make beautiful juicy meat.

4 Enjoy with just about everything, whether it's a light salad or sandwich rolls with BBQ sauce and salad.

CHEFS NOTE

Pulled pork is an absolute classic. It's a chance to use almost everything in your spice rack to create a 'killer' dry rub and it always packs an irresistible punchy and more-ish taste.

SAUSAGE & SPINACH WITH GNOCCHI

309 calories per serving

Ingredients

- 6 lean, pork or beef sausages (skins removed)
- 250ml/1 cup passata/sieved tomatoes
- 1 tsp dried rosemary
- 1 splash red wine vinegar
- ½ tsp salt

- 1 400g/14oz tin chopped tomatoes
- 2 tbsp tomato puree
- ½ tsp brown sugar
- 100g/ 3 ½ oz fresh spinach
- 500g/1lb 2oz gnocchi

Method

1 Brown the sausage meat in a frying pan and break up well. Add all the ingredients, except the gnocchi and spinach, to the slow cooker and combine. Close the lid tightly and leave to cook on high for 3-4 hours.

2 When the meat is well cooked, stir in the fresh spinach, gnocchi and leave to cook for a further 10-20 mins or until the gnocchi is tender.

CHEFS NOTE

This lovely recipe uses sausage meat to create a thick, luxurious sauce which is just perfect with freshly cooked gnocchi. You can also add some crushed chilli if you prefer a 'kick' of heat.

COWBOY CASSEROLE

414 calories per serving

Ingredients

- 8 lean pork sausages
- 2 400g/14oz tins mixed beans, drained
- 2 400g/14oz tins chopped tomatoes
- 1 onion, chopped
- 2 carrots, chopped
- 1 tbsp tomato puree/paste or ketchup
- 1 tsp brown sugar
- 1 tsp Dijon/mild mustard
- Low cal cooking spray

Method

1 Brown the sausages in the pan with the onions. Combine all the ingredients in the slow cooker and leave to cook for 3-4 hours on high or low for 5-6 hours with the lid tightly shut.

2 Check the sausages are properly cooked through and, if you want to thicken the sauce up, leave the lid off while you cook on high for up to 45 mins extra.

3 Serve on its own with crusty bread or with mashed potato and green veg.

CHEFS NOTE
Loved by kids and adults alike, this is a real cowboy's supper-time meal which always goes down a treat. It takes just minutes to put together and is a great way to get some vegetables into the kids.

AROMATIC KICKING PORK RIBS

448 calories per serving

Ingredients

- 1kg/2¼ lbs pork ribs
- 1 tsp each garlic powder, chilli, cumin & basil
- ½ tsp salt

- 2 400g/14oz tins chopped tomatoes
- 1 tbsp ketchup
- 1 green chilli, chopped or a pinch of crushed chilli flakes to taste

Method

1 Rub the dry spices onto the ribs. Add all the ingredients to the slow cooker and leave to cook with the lid tightly on for 5-6 hours on low.

2 Ensure the ribs are super tender and serve with rice and beans.

CHEFS NOTE

There are a number of different types of rib available depending on the cut from which they are taken. Choose whichever is cheapest or whichever you prefer. All will work well with this recipe.

SWEET & SOUR PINEAPPLE PORK

238 calories per serving

Ingredients

- 900g/2lb lean cubed pork
- 1 tbsp plain/all purpose flour
- 1 400g/14oz tin pineapple chunks (reserve the juice)
- 1 onion, chopped
- 1 green (bell) pepper, chopped
- 2 carrots, cut into batons
- 1 tbsp brown sugar
- ½ tsp salt
- 2 tbsp lime juice
- 1 tbsp light soy sauce
- 120ml/½ cup vegetable stock/broth
- Low cal cooking spray

Method

1 Brown the pork in a frying pan with a little low cal spray. Remove from the pan and dust with the flour. Put all the other ingredients, except the pineapple chunks, into the slow cooker (include the pineapple juice).

2 Combine everything and leave to cook on low for 4-5 hours with the lid tightly closed.

3 Check the pork is tender and then add the pineapple chunks. Leave for a further 30 min and serve with boiled rice.

CHEFS NOTE

Sweet and sour is one of the most loved Chinese meals in the world. This is not supposed to be an authentic copy - just take it as a super simple replica which should satisfy your eastern cravings.

CUMIN PORK & KIDNEY BEANS

366 calories per serving

Ingredients

- 1 400g/14oz tin kidney beans, drained
- 300g/11oz lean boneless pork shoulder, cubed
- 1 onion, chopped
- 4 garlic cloves, crushed
- 1 tsp sunflower oil
- 1 tsp ground cumin
- ½ tsp turmeric
- 250ml/1 cup vegetable stock/broth
- Salt & pepper to taste

Method

1 Quickly brown the cubed pork in a frying pan with the sunflower oil.

2 Add all the ingredients to the slow cooker and season well. Cover and leave to cook on high for 3-4 hours or low for 5-6 hours, or until the pork is tender and cooked through. If you want to thicken the sauce a little, leave the lid off and cook for an additional 45 mins, or until you have the consistency you prefer.

CHEFS NOTE
This pork dish is great served with rice and sour cream. You could also garnish with some fresh finely chopped chillies.

LENTILS, SAUSAGES & PEAS

390
calories per
serving

Ingredients

- 50g/2oz red lentils
- ½ tsp each crushed chilli flakes, ground cumin & coriander/cilantro
- 1 onion, sliced
- 450g/1lb lean pork sausages
- 120ml/ ½ cup beef stock/broth

- 150g/5oz frozen peas
- 1 tbsp Dijon mustard
- 2 tbsp freshly chopped flat leaf parsley
- Low cal cooking spray
- Salt & pepper to taste

Method

1 Add a little low cal spray to a frying pan and quickly brown the sausages. Add all the ingredients to the slow cooker, stir well, cover and leave to cook on high for 2-3 hours or low for 4-5 hours. If you need more liquid during cooking add a little more stock.

2 Ensure the lentils are tender and the sausages cooked through. Serve with boiled potatoes and spinach.

CHEFS NOTE
You can serve the sausages whole or alternatively remove after cooking, slice in diagonals, return to the slow cooker and stir through before serving.

SLOW COOKER
LAMB DISHES

LAMB PILAU PAZAR

400
calories per
serving

Ingredients

- 500g/1lb 2oz lean lamb cut into bite sized chunks (any lean cut will work for this recipe)
- 1 large onion, chopped
- 1 carrot, chopped
- 1 stick celery, chopped
- 1 400g/14oz tin chopped tomatoes
- 1 tsp dried crushed chilli flakes

- 150g/5oz brown rice
- 500ml/2 cups vegetable stock/broth
- 1 cinnamon stick or ½ tsp ground cinnamon
- 1 tbsp chopped, dried apricots or raisins
- Salt & pepper to taste
- Low cal cooking spray

Method

1 Gently sauté the onion in a little low cal spray, remove from the pan and then brown off the lamb for a couple of minutes on a high heat. Combine all the ingredients together in the slow cooker, except the rice. Cover and cook on low for 4-6 hours, add the rice and cook for 30 mins or until the rice and lamb are both tender and cooked through.

2 If any additional liquid remains, cook on a high heat with the lid off for a further 45 minutes or until the liquid is absorbed into the rice.

3 If you want to add garnish serve with toasted pine nuts, chopped coriander/cilantro or crushed almonds.

CHEFS NOTE
Also known as pilaf, Pilau is a rice based dish now common just about everywhere. The version here has a taste of the Turkish to it hence its title Pazar which means 'Sunday' and is also the name of a beautiful coastal village in the Rize province of the country.

SPINACH & LAMB STEW

467 calories per serving

Ingredients

- 500g/1lb 2oz lean lamb cut into bite sized chunks (any lean cut will work)
- 2 cloves garlic, crushed
- Zest of 1 lemon
- 1 onion, chopped
- 2 400g/14oz tins chopped tomatoes
- 1 tbsp tomato puree/paste
- 1 400g/14oz tin chickpeas, drained

- 400g/14oz fresh spinach, chopped
- Dried herb mix of the following:
- 1 tsp each coriander/cilantro & turmeric
- ½ tsp each ground cumin, black pepper & oregano
- 2 tbsp low fat Greek yoghurt
- Salt & pepper to taste
- Low cal cooking spray

Method

1 Gently sauté the onion in a little low cal oil, remove from the pan and then brown the lamb for a couple of minutes on a high heat.

2 Combine all ingredients together (except the yoghurt and spinach) in the slow cooker with the lid tightly shut and cook on low for 4-6 hours or until the lamb is tender and cooked through.

3 30mins before the end of cooking add the spinach, stir through the yoghurt before serving.

CHEFS NOTE

Super rich in iron & calcium, spinach is a super-food which is twinned beautifully in this dish with chickpeas, lemon zest and Greek inspired spices.

MARRAKESH LAMB

415 calories per serving

Ingredients

- 500g/1lb 2oz trimmed lamb cut into cubes (any lean cut will work)
- ½ tsp black pepper
- 1 tsp each ground cumin, coriander, ginger, turmeric & paprika
- 1 tsp cinnamon
- 2 400g/14oz tins chopped tomatoes
- 75g/3oz red split lentils
- 1 lt/4 cups lamb stock/broth or boiling water
- 2 onions, chopped
- 1 tsp brown sugar
- 5 cloves garlic, crushed

Method

1 This one couldn't be any easier. No need to brown the meat, so just combine all the ingredients in the slow cooker, cover and leave to cook on low for 4-6 hours. Ensure the lamb is tender and cooked through. If you want to thicken up a little, leave to cook for a further 45 mins with the lid off.

2 Delicious served with low fat Greek yoghurt, couscous or fragrant rice.

CHEFS NOTE
Morocco's capital is world renowned for its tagine cuisine. Slow cookers provide a wonderful alternative to this specialist style of cooking. This recipe is a lovely North African inspired dish which, if its new to you, should piqué your interest in Moroccan cooking.

SERVES 4

LAMB & SAAG SPINACH

320
calories per
serving

Ingredients

- 500g/1lb 2oz lean lamb shoulder, cubed
- 1 tsp each fenugreek & mustard seeds
- 1 tsp each ground cumin & ginger
- 2 cloves garlic, crushed
- 250ml/1 cup beef stock/broth
- 400g/14oz spinach
- 120ml/½ cup fat free Greek yoghurt
- 1 tsp mint sauce (shop bought)

Method

1 Other than the yoghurt and mint sauce add all the ingredients to the slow cooker, cover and leave to cook on low for 4-6 hours or until the lamb is tender.

2 Stir the yoghurt and mint sauce through and serve straight away.

CHEFS NOTE
Saag means 'leaf' dish in Indian cuisine. You could try out other green leaves as an alternative to spinach if you prefer.

LOSE WEIGHT FOR GOOD
SLOW COOKER DIET
FOR BEGINNERS

SLOW COOKER SEAFOOD DISHES

· ·

SERVES 4

GREEN THAI FISH CURRY

215 calories per serving

Ingredients

- 500g/1lb 2oz meaty white fish fillets (go for whatever is on sale) haddock, cod, Pollock or cobbler
- 3 onions, chopped
- 1 tsp fresh ginger or ½ tsp ground ginger
- 3 cloves garlic, crushed
- 150g/5oz green beans
- 1 red chilli, chopped
- 50g/2oz watercress
- 2 tbsp Thai green curry paste
- 500ml/2 cups low fat coconut milk
- Low cal cooking spray
- Salt & pepper to taste

Method

1 Sauté the onions & green beans with the ginger and garlic over a low heat in a little low cal spray. Season the fish fillets and carefully combine all the ingredients (except the watercress) in the slow cooker. Cook on low for 1 ½ hours with the lid tightly shut. This timing should mean your fish is not overcooked and the green beans have some bite to them.

2 Check the fish is properly cooked through by flaking it a little with a fork and gently add the watercress salad to the mix before serving. Serve with noodles or rice.

3 If you want to make it a little spicier you could add some more chopped chilli or crushed chilli flakes.

CHEFS NOTE
Compared to meat, fish cooks more quickly in the slow cooker and as such fish recipes can be really handy if you haven't got too much cooking time. This recipe is a fantastic and easy Thai curry which is simple to prepare and doesn't take long at all in the slow cooker.

54

SWEET & CITRUS SALMON

270 calories per serving

Ingredients

- 500g/1lb 2oz thick boneless salmon fillets
- 1 onion, chopped
- 1 tbsp light soy sauce
- Juice of 1 fresh lime or 3 tbsp Lime juice
- 2 garlic cloves, crushed
- 1 tsp sugar dissolved into 3 tbsp warm water and brushed onto the fillets
- Low cal cooking spray
- Salt & pepper to taste

Method

1 Chop the onion and sauté for a couple of minutes with the garlic in a little low cal oil. Remove from the pan and carefully combine all the ingredients in the slow cooker. Cook on low for 1½ hours with the lid tightly on.

2 Check the fish is properly cooked by flaking it a little with a fork and serve with salad potatoes and carrots. Alternatively, use in a lovely warm salad served with a little crusty bread.

CHEFS NOTE
Salmon can be relatively expensive so you can substitute for tilapia or basa or talk to your fishmonger for recommendations.

TUNA & NOODLE CATTIA

250 calories per serving

Ingredients

- 350g/12oz fresh egg noodles
- 1 onion, chopped
- 1 400g/14oz tin fat free condensed mushroom soup
- 2 200g/7oz tins tuna steaks or flakes in water
- 100g/3½ oz frozen peas
- 1 tsp garlic powder
- Salt & pepper to taste
- Pinch of crushed chilli flakes

Method

1 Quickly cook the noodles in salted boiling water. Save 3 tbsp of the drained water and then combine all the ingredients and saved water in the slow cooker. Cover and leave to cook on low for 1½ hours.

2 This is great served with a sliced red onion & tomato salad and a little parmesan.

CHEFS NOTE

An absolute classic American slow cooker recipe, Tuna & Noodle casserole is always a winner. This version takes it back to basics using the simplest store cupboard ingredients. The title 'Cattia' pays homage to the ancient Latin roots where the word 'casserole' has its origins.

CORIANDER & GARLIC PRAWNS

269 calories per serving

Ingredients

- 500g/1lb 2oz raw king prawns
- 200g/7oz frozen peas
- 1 tsp sunflower oil
- 2 onions, sliced
- 200g/8oz cherry tomatoes, halved
- 1 tsp ground ginger
- 4 garlic cloves, crushed
- 3 tbsp curry paste
- 2 tbsp fresh chopped coriander/cilantro + extra for garnish
- 250ml/1 cup passata/sieved tomatoes
- Salt & pepper to taste

Method

1 Add all the ingredients to the slow cooker, cover and leave to cook on low for 1-2 hours or until the prawns are cooked through and the peas are tender.

2 Sprinkle with chopped coriander and serve with rice.

CHEFS NOTE

This is a really simple 'cheat' curry using curry paste. If you want a slightly different taste you could use less passata and add a little coconut milk to the recipe after cooking.

FISH STEW

245
calories per serving

Ingredients

- 450g/1lb white fish fillets, cubed
- 1 leek, chopped
- 4 garlic cloves, crushed
- 1 400g/14oz tin chopped tomatoes
- 100g/3½ oz frozen peas
- 2 celery stalks, chopped

- 1 onion chopped
- ½ tsp fennel seeds
- 1 tbsp dried basil
- 1lt/4 cups fish stock/broth
- 250g/9oz raw prawns
- Salt & Pepper to taste

Method

1 Mix together all the ingredients, except the fish, peas and prawns in the slow cooker. Season, cover and leave to cook on low for 4-5 hours or high for 2-3 hours.

2 Meanwhile season the fish and prawns. 45 mins before the end of cooking add the fish, prawns and peas. Continue to cook until the seafood is cooked right through and the peas are tender.

3 Serve with noodles as a soup stew.

CHEFS NOTE
Feel free to use any type of meaty white fish you like and, if you feel adventurous, you could add some squid, octopus or clams to the stew.

FRESH MACKEREL & SUMMER SEASON PEPPERS

190 calories per serving

Ingredients

- 2 yellow or orange peppers, sliced
- 2 onions, sliced
- 1 garlic clove, crushed
- 1 red chilli, finely sliced
- 250ml/1 cup fish stock
- 400g/14oz fresh whole mackerel, gutted
- 200g/7oz ripe plum tomatoes, chopped
- 2 tbsp tomato puree
- 200g/7oz rocket
- Low cal cooking oil spray
- Salt & pepper to taste

Method

1 Gently sauté the peppers, onions, garlic & chilli in a little low cal spray until softened.

2 Add the sautéed vegetables to the slow cooker along with all the other ingredients, except the rocket.

3 Gently combine, cover and leave to cook on low for 4-6 hours or until the fish is tender and cooked through.

4 Gently lift out of the slow cooker (try to keep the fish whole), season and serve with the rocket leaves.

CHEFS NOTE
Use yellow or orange peppers rather than un-ripened green peppers.

FRESH HERBED SALMON

250 calories per serving

Ingredients

- 500g/1lb 2oz boneless salmon fillets
- 250ml/1 cup fish stock
- 4 tbsp freshly chopped flat leaf parsley
- 4 tbsp freshly chopped basil
- 3 tbsp low fat mayonnaise

- Lemon wedges to serve
- 200g/7oz mixed green salad leaves
- Low cal cooking oil spray
- Salt & pepper to taste

Method

1 Place the salmon, stock and half the chopped herbs in the slow cooker. Gently combine, cover and leave to cook on high for 1-2 hours or until the fish is tender and cooked through.

2 Mix the rest of the chopped herbs together with the mayonnaise, a squeeze of lemon and some salt & pepper.

3 Remove the salmon fillets from the slow cooker.

4 Spread the herbed mayonnaise onto the salmon fillets and serve with salad leaves and lemon wedges to serve.

CHEFS NOTE
You can alter the mix of fresh herbs to suit your own taste. Chives and coriander make a good alternative.

CARIBBEAN SPICED SCALLOPS

200 calories per serving

Ingredients

- 200g/7oz ripe plum tomatoes, roughly chopped
- 500g/1lb 2oz prepared fresh scallops
- 250ml/1 cup fish stock
- ½ tsp each ground all spice, chilli powder, coriander/cilantro & paprika

- 1 bunch spring onions/scallions roughly chopped
- 2 large romaine lettuces, shredded
- 2 red peppers, sliced
- Low cal cooking oil spray
- Salt & pepper to taste

Method

1 First gently sauté the peppers & plum tomatoes in a little low cal oil for a few minutes until softened.

2 Place the scallops, stock, dried spices, spring onions, sautéed peppers & plum tomatoes in the slow cooker.

3 Gently combine, cover and leave to cook on high for 45 minutes - 1 hour or until the scallops are cooked through.

4 Gently lift the scallops, tomatoes & peppers out of the slow cooker.

5 Season and serve with the shredded lettuce.

CHEFS NOTE
Sweet potato mash makes a great side to this Caribbean dish.

LIME SHRIMPS WITH BABY SPINACH LEAVES & RICE

280 calories per serving

Ingredients

- 500g/1lb 2oz raw shelled king prawns
- 250ml/1 cup low fat coconut milk
- 2 tbsp lime juice
- 1 tbsp Thai fish sauce
- 1 tsp brown sugar
- 1 red chilli, finely sliced

- 200g/7oz baby spinach leaves
- 4 tbsp freshly chopped coriander/cilantro
- 200g/7oz long grain rice
- Low cal cooking oil spray
- Salt & pepper to taste

Method

1 Place the prawns, coconut milk, lime juice, fish sauce, sugar, chilli & spinach in the slow cooker.

2 Gently combine, cover and leave to cook on high for 45 minutes - 1 hour or until the prawns are cooked through.

3 Meanwhile cook the rice in salted boiling water until tender.

4 Serve the prawns and coconut milk on top of the drained rice with freshly chopped coriander sprinkled on top.

CHEFS NOTE
Spinach is in season throughout late spring and summer. Baby leaves are the most sweet and tender.

PINEAPPLE CURRY PRAWNS WITH SUGAR SNAP PEAS

360 calories per serving

Ingredients

- 1 onion, sliced
- 2 garlic cloves, crushed
- 500g/1lb 2oz raw shelled king prawns
- 250ml/1 cup low fat coconut milk
- 1 tbsp medium curry powder
- 1 tbsp lime juice
- 1 tbsp Thai fish sauce

- 2 tbsp tomato puree
- 200g/7oz fresh or tinned pineapple, roughly chopped
- 200g/7oz sugar snap peas
- 200g/7oz fine egg noodles
- Low cal cooking oil spray
- Salt & pepper to taste

Method

1 Gently sauté the onions & garlic in a little low cal oil for a few minutes until softened. Then place in the slow cooker.

2 Add the prawns, coconut milk, curry powder, lime juice, fish sauce, tomato puree, pineapple & peas in the slow cooker.

3 Gently combine, cover and leave to cook on high for 1-2 hours or until the prawns are cooked through.

4 Meanwhile cook the noodles in salted boiling water until tender.

5 Mix the drained noodles, prawns and sauce together & serve.

CHEFS NOTE
You could serve the sugar snaps peas roughly chopped and raw in this lovely summer noodle dish if you prefer.

SLOW COOKER
VEGETARIAN DISHES

POMODORO PASTA SAUCE

122
calories per serving

Ingredients

- 2 400g/14oz tins chopped tomatoes
- 6 large fresh tomatoes (vine ripened are best)
- 250ml/1 cup passata/sieved tomatoes
- Handful sliced black olives
- Bunch fresh basil chopped (reserve a little some for garnish)
- 3 garlic cloves, crushed
- 1 onion, chopped
- 1 tsp brown sugar
- 1 tsp extra virgin olive oil
- Salt and pepper to taste

Method

1 Combine all the ingredients in the slow cooker and cover. Leave to cook on low for 5-6 hours or high for 3-4 hours. Delicious served with angel hair pasta, salad & grated parmesan cheese.

CHEFS NOTE

This is a simple tomato based Italian sauce which gets better the longer you leave it. Reheated leftovers often have a greater depth of taste which is worth waiting for.

VEGGIE TURMERIC CHICKPEAS

234 calories per serving

Ingredients

- 2 400g/14oz tins chickpeas, drained
- 2 onions, chopped
- 1 tbsp tomato puree/paste
- 2 cloves garlic, crushed
- 1 tsp fresh grated ginger or ½ teaspoon ground ginger
- 2 tsp garam masala
- 1 tsp each ground cumin & coriander/cilantro
- 2 tsp turmeric
- ½ tsp chilli powder
- 200g/7oz fresh spinach
- 3 tbsp lemon juice
- 250ml/1 cup veg stock/broth
- Salt & pepper to taste

Method

1 Combine all the ingredients, except the lemon juice and spinach, in the slow cooker. Cook on low for 5-6 hours or on high for 3-4 hours with the lid tightly shut. Add a little more stock during cooking if needed.

2 Ensure the chickpeas are cooked though, stir in the lemon juice and spinach. Serve with rice and naan bread.

CHEFS NOTE
Chickpeas have been used in cooking for many hundreds of years. The spinach in this recipe will be crunchy, if you prefer your spinach well cooked, add earlier during cooking.

TOMATO & GARLIC MUSHROOMS

180 calories per serving

Ingredients

- 1 tbsp olive oil
- 450g/1lb chestnut mushrooms
- 5 cloves garlic, crushed
- 1 stick celery
- 1 400g/14oz tin chopped tomatoes
- 1 tbsp tomato puree/paste
- 3 tbsp fresh chopped flat leaf parsley
- ½ tsp crushed chilli flakes
- 1 onion, chopped

Method

1 Add all the ingredients to the slow cooker, except the parsley. Season, cover and leave to cook on high for 3-4 hours or low for 5-6 hours or until the mushrooms are tender and the flavours have thoroughly blended.

CHEFS NOTE
This is great served with spaghetti & salad for a delicious Italian meal, or on bruschetta as a snack.

FENNEL RISOTTO

Ingredients

- 1 fennel bulb, diced
- 250g/9oz risotto rice
- 1 carrot, chopped
- 1 onion, chopped
- 25g/1oz grated parmesan cheese
- 50g/2oz black olives, finely chopped
- 3 garlic cloves, crushed
- 1lt/4 cups vegetable stock/broth
- 125g/4oz frozen peas
- 50g/2oz rocket
- 15g/ ½ oz butter
- Salt & pepper to taste

Method

1 Preheat the slow cooker and place the butter in the bottom. When it is melted, add the risotto rice and stir well until every grain is finely coated. Add the rest of the ingredients, except the cheese and rocket, to the slow cooker and season well. Cover and leave to cook on high for 2-3 hours. If you need to add more liquid during cooking go ahead by adding just a little each time.

2 After cooking, all the liquid should be absorbed and the rice should be tender. If it isn't, leave to cook for a little longer with the lid off.

3 Serve sprinkled with parmesan cheese and the rocket piled on top.

CHEFS NOTE
Risotto usually needs a lot of stirring during cooking. This slow cooker alternative is a great labour saver with virtually no stirring required.

WILD MUSHROOM STROGANOFF

101 calories per serving

Ingredients

- 500g/1lb 2oz wild mixed mushrooms sliced
- 2 onions, chopped
- 4 garlic cloves, crushed
- 2 tsp smoked paprika

- 250ml/1 cup vegetable stock/broth
- 1 400g/14oz tin low fat condensed mushroom soup
- Bunch flat chopped leaf parsley (reserve a little for garnish)

Method

1 Add all the ingredients into the slow cooker. Close the lid tightly and leave to cook on high for 2-3 hours or low for 4-5 hours. Ensure the mushrooms are tender and serve with pasta or rice and a spoon of fat free Greek yoghurt.

CHEFS NOTE

The more exciting the mushrooms the better this dish is going to taste. Use whatever you can get your hands on but a combination of portobello, shitake, morel, oyster and enoki would be fantastic. However don't be put off if you can only get regular varieties - it will still taste good!

BEAN, POTATO & CHEESE STEW

434 calories per serving

Ingredients

- 1 400g/14oz tin sweetcorn
- 2 400g/14oz tins mixed beans, drained
- 1 red (bell) pepper, chopped
- 1 onion, chopped
- 500ml/2 cups passata/sieved tomatoes
- 1 tsp each cumin & coriander/cilantro
- Salt & pepper to taste
- 125g/4oz grated low fat cheese
- 125g/4oz potatoes, diced & peeled
- ½ tsp cayenne pepper
- Juice of one lemon or 2tbsp lemon juice

Method

1 Add all the ingredients to the slow cooker, except the cheese. Combine well and sprinkle the cheese onto the top. Cook on low for 5-6 hours or on high for 3-4 hours with the lid tightly shut.

2 Make sure the potatoes are tender and serve with sour cream and flat bread. If you find the stew is a little dry during cooking, add some water to loosen.

CHEFS NOTE
This vegetarian meal is a lovely Mexican inspired dish which is so hearty, you won't miss the meat at all. Feel free to spice it up with extra cayenne pepper if you like and serve with an onion & tomato or green salad.

LENTIL DHAL

160
calories per
serving

Ingredients

- 400g/14oz split red lentils
- 1 onion, chopped
- 1 garlic clove, crushed
- 1 tsp each ground coriander/cilantro, turmeric & cumin
- ½ each tsp ground ginger, paprika & mustard seeds

- 500ml/2 cups vegetable stock/broth
- 2 tbsp freshly chopped coriander/ cilantro
- 25g/1oz butter
- Salt & pepper to taste

Method

1 Add all the ingredients, except corriander to the slow cooker, cover and leave to cook on low for 4-6 hours or until the lentils are tender and the liquid absorbed. Add a little more stock or water during cooking if needed. If there is too much liquid, take the lid off and leave to cook on high for approx 40 mins.

2 Sprinkle the chopped coriander over the top and serve.

CHEFS NOTE
Dhal is a one of the most common dishes in Asia. It is eaten by some families at almost every single meal time. This simple version is great served with Indian chapatti bread.

BUTTER BEAN & ALMOND STEW

206 calories per serving

Ingredients

- 1 onion, sliced into rounds
- 2 garlic cloves, crushed
- 300g/11oz new potatoes, sliced
- 1 tsp mustard seeds
- 2 tbsp tomato puree/paste
- ½ tsp ground cinnamon
- 1 celery stick, chopped

- 450g/1lb cauliflower florets
- 50g/2oz sultanas
- 200g/7oz tinned butter beans, drained
- 50g/2oz chopped almonds
- 1 400g/14oz tin chopped tomatoes
- 250ml/1 cup vegetable stock/broth
- Salt & pepper to taste

Method

1 Add all the ingredients to the slow cooker, cover, stir well and leave to cook on high for 2-3 hours or low for 4-5 hours or until the vegetables are tender.

CHEFS NOTE

If you want the stew a little thicker, take the lid off and continue to cook on high for 45mins or until the consistency is to your liking.

SLOW COOKER
SOUP DISHES

HOCK HAM & SPLIT PEA SOUP

178
calories per serving

Ingredients

- 2 ham knuckles (get them smoked if you can)
- 3 carrots, chopped
- 2 celery stalks, chopped
- 1 onion chopped
- 3 garlic cloves, crushed
- 500g/1lb 2oz green split peas (yellow or green are fine)
- 1 ½ lt/6 cups chicken stock/broth

Method

1 Combine all the ingredients into the slow cooker and cook on low for 5-6 hours or high for 3-4 hours with the lid tightly shut. When the soup is cooked, take out the hocks and strip the meat - if they are fully cooked the meat should fall away easily.

2 Discard any fat and stir the shredded ham back into the soup. If you want to alter the texture you can thicken it up by mashing the split peas a little before putting the ham back in.

CHEFS NOTE
Ham hocks are a bargain ingredient that can give a real depth to a dish. You could substitute ham hocks for a meaty ham bone if you had one left after a family gathering.

SUPER SIMPLE CHICKEN TACO SOUP

247 calories per serving

Ingredients

- 125g/4oz skinless chicken breast
- 1 400g/14oz tin sweetcorn
- 1 400g/14oz tin black beans, drained
- 1 400g/14oz tin kidney bean, drained
- 1 400g/14oz tin chopped tomatoes
- 2 cloves garlic, crushed
- 1 ¼lt/5 cups chicken stock/broth
- 1 red chilli, chopped

- 4 tsp taco seasoning
Or make your own:
- 1 tsp chilli powder, 1 ½ tsp ground cumin, ½ tsp paprika, ¼ tsp each of onion powder, garlic powder, dried oregano & crushed chilli flakes, 1 tsp each of sea salt & black pepper

Method

1 Season the chicken breast and place at the bottom of the slow cooker. Add all the other ingredients and leave to cook for 2 hours on high or 3 hours on low with the lid tightly shut. Ensure the chicken is cooked through and tender then shred it a little with 2 forks through the soup.

2 If you want to thicken the soup up after cooking, take the lid off and cook on high for a further 45 minutes or until you get the consistency you want.

3 Serve with tortilla chips, crusty bread or over rice depending on how much of a meal you want to make of it.

CHEFS NOTE
No one knows when Taco turned into soup, but whenever it was it has become a firm favourite which is worth celebrating in the slow cooker.

SQUASH, BASIL & TOMATO SOUP

130 calories per serving

Ingredients

- 400g/14oz butternut squash flesh, cubed
- 75g/3oz potatoes, peeled & cubed
- 8 fresh vine tomatoes, chopped
- ½ tsp sugar
- 2 tbsp freshly chopped basil leaves
- 4 tbsp tomato puree/paste
- 1lt/4 cups vegetable stock/broth
- 60ml/¼ cup single cream
- Salt & pepper to taste

Method

1 Place all the ingredients, except the cream, in the slow cooker. Season, cover and leave to cook on low for 3-4 hours or until the vegetables are tender.

2 After cooking blend the soup to a smooth consistency and serve with a swirl of fresh cream.

CHEFS NOTE

Butternut squash is a perfect slow cooker ingredient. Its creamy, firm texture holds well during cooking and forms a robust base to this tasty soup.

SPANISH SAUSAGE SOUP

140 calories per serving

Ingredients

- 75g/3oz potatoes, cubed
- 450g/1lb cauliflower florets, finely chopped
- 1 tbsp olive oil
- 750ml/3 cups vegetable stock/broth
- 250ml/1 cup semi skimmed milk
- 2 tbsp freshly chopped flat leaf parsley
- 1 tsp smoked paprika
- 100g/3½ oz chorizo sausage, finely chopped
- Salt & pepper to taste

Method

1 Place all the ingredients, except the parsley, in the slow cooker. Season, cover and leave to cook on low for 3-4 hours or until the vegetables are tender.

2 Adjust the seasoning and serve with the parsley sprinkled on top.

CHEFS NOTE
Chorizo sausage is quintessentially Spanish. You can use either the cooked, cured or raw versions of chorizo for this recipe.

ST.PATRICK'S DAY SOUP

100 calories per serving

Ingredients

- 300g/11oz potatoes chopped
- 1 onion, chopped
- 3 leeks, chopped

- Salt & pepper to taste
- 500ml/2 cups skimmed milk
- 750ml/3 cups vegetable stock/broth

Method

1 Combine all the ingredients together in the slow cooker and leave to cook on low for 4-5 hours with the lid tightly shut. Make sure the potatoes are tender, season to taste and then either blend as a smooth soup or eat it rough, ready and rustic with some crusty bread.

2 You can also add a garnish of chopped chives and sour cream or crème fraiche if you want to add an extra touch.

CHEFS NOTE
It's often said that everyone is Irish on St. Patrick's day, here's a chance to get a real taste of Ireland every day with this lovely Irish inspired potato soup.

SPICY CARROT SOUP

247 calories per serving

Ingredients

- 2 tsp ground cumin
- ½ tsp crushed chilli flakes
- 1 tbsp olive oil
- 750g/1lb 11oz carrots, finely chopped
- ½ onion, finely chopped

- 140g/4½ oz split red lentils
- 750ml/3 cups vegetable stock/broth
- 120ml/½ cup milk
- 60ml/¼ cup single cream
- Salt & pepper to taste.

Method

1 Add all the ingredients to the slow cooker, except the cream and milk. Season, cover and leave to cook on high for approx 3 hours or until the lentils are tender.

2 Add the milk and warm through for a minute or two. Use a food processor or blender to whizz the soup to a smooth consistency and serve with a swirl of single cream in each bowl.

CHEFS NOTE

This warming soup can be tweaked to suit your taste - add more or less chilli flakes as you prefer. Plus if you want to reduce the calories a little, swap the olive oil for low cal cooking spray and the regular milk for skimmed.

FLAGEOLET & SAVOY SOUP

220 calories per serving

Ingredients

- 1 onion, finely chopped
- 1 carrot, finely chopped
- 1 whole savoy cabbage, chopped
- 1 tbsp olive oil
- 1lt/4 cups vegetable stock/broth

- 2 tbsp tomato puree/paste
- 1 tsp each dried oregano & rosemary
- Salt & Pepper to taste
- 1 400g/14oz tin flageolet beans, drained

Method

1 Place all the ingredients in the slow cooker. Season, cover and leave to cook on low for 3-4 hours or until the vegetables are tender. Adjust the seasoning and serve.

CHEFS NOTE

This soup is best served chunky. If however, you prefer a smoother consistency, reserve a ladle of flageolet beans from the cooked soup, blend the rest of the soup and stir the whole beans back through before serving.

PARSNIP & COCONUT MILK SOUP

238 calories per serving

Ingredients

- 1 onion, chopped
- 4 parsnips, chopped
- 4 carrots, chopped
- 1 tsp each turmeric, cumin, coriander/ cilantro & paprika
- 120ml/½ cup low fat coconut milk
- 2 tbsp freshly chopped chives
- 750ml/3 cups vegetable stock/broth
- Salt & pepper to taste
- 250ml/1 cup fat free Greek yoghurt

Method

1 Place all the ingredients, except the chives, coconut milk & yoghurt in the slow cooker. Season, cover and leave to cook on low for 3-4 hours or until the vegetables are tender.

2 After cooking, blend the soup to a smooth consistency. Stor through the coconut milk and serve with a dollop of yoghurt in the middle and some fresh chives sprinkled on top.

CHEFS NOTE
Adding the coconut milk during lengthy cooking risks the milk 'splitting', so leave it until the end and warm through.

CORN & POTATO CHOWDER

230
calories per serving

Ingredients

- 1 onion, chopped
- 400g/14oz sweetcorn
- 400g/14oz creamed sweetcorn
- 2 cloves garlic, crushed
- 750ml/3 cups chicken or vegetable stock/broth

- 350g/12oz potatoes, diced
- 1 tsp low fat 'butter' spread
- 500ml/2 cups semi skimmed milk
- Salt & pepper to taste
- Low cal cooking spray

Method

1 Gently sauté the onion and garlic in a little low cal spray. Place all the ingredients in the slow cooker and cook on low for 3-4 hours with the lid tightly shut.

2 Ensure the potatoes are tender and mash a little with a fork to create the right consistency.

3 Serve with saltine or cream crackers for an authentic finish.

CHEFS NOTE

Although primarily associated with seafood, chowder is a lovely thick soup recipe which works just as well with vegetables alone. You could easily add some smoked haddock to this recipe if you wanted to be authentic, but this veggie option is good too.

SPINACH & HARICOT SOUP

240
calories per serving

Ingredients

- 2 lt/8 cups vegetable stock/broth
- 4 tbsp tomato puree/paste
- 1 400g/14oz tin haricot beans, rinsed
- 250g/9oz brown rice
- 200g/7oz spinach
- 2 onions, chopped
- 2 garlic cloves, crushed
- 1 tsp each dried basil & oregano
- Salt & pepper to taste

Method

1 Combine all the ingredients, except the spinach, into the slow cooker. Season, cover and leave to cook on low for 5-6 hours or high for 3-4 hours. 20 minutes before the end of cooking, stir through the spinach.

2 Serve with crusty bread.

CHEFS NOTE
This hearty soup is great freshened up with a twist of lemon and chopped basil to garnish.

SLOW COOKER
BREAKFASTS

•••

SPANISH TORTILLA

396 calories per serving

Ingredients

- A dozen eggs, gently fork whisked
- One large onion, chopped
- 150g/5oz potatoes, peeled and cut into thin slices
- 50g/2oz cured chorizo Spanish sausage, finely chopped
- Salt & pepper to taste
- Low cal cooking spray

Method

1 Gently sauté the onions and potatoes in a little low cal spray until golden (5-10 mins). Spray the slow cooker with a little more oil and add all the ingredients.

2 Combine well, cover and leave to cook on low overnight for 6-8 hours for a perfect morning feast.

CHEFS NOTE

This Spanish omelette makes a fantastic hearty start to the morning. It's also great served cold and cut into slices with a fresh green salad.

MORNING RISOTTO

271 calories per serving

Ingredients

- 175g/6oz risotto rice
- 4 apples, peeled, cored & sliced
- 125g/4oz sultanas
- 1 tsp cinnamon
- ½ tsp nutmeg

- ¼ tsp ground cloves
- 500ml/2 cups water
- 500ml/2 cups skimmed milk
- 1 tbsp brown sugar
- Knob butter

Method

1 Melt the butter in a pan and add the rice. Make sure it's all nicely coated for just a minute or two and then add all the ingredients to the slow cooker.

2 Leave to cook overnight for 6-8 hours with the lid tightly closed. If it feels a little stodgy in the morning loosen it up by stirring a dash of cold milk through.

CHEFS NOTE
Another lovely breakfast alternative which uses Italian rice to give the dish its base.

FRUIT GRANOLA

300 calories per serving

Ingredients

- 500g/1lb 2oz plain granola cereal
- 100g/3 ½ oz oatmeal
- 1 tsp cinnamon
- ½ tsp nutmeg
- 1 tbsp runny honey
- 4 apples sliced & cored
- 50g/2oz sultanas
- 50g/2oz low fat 'butter' spread, melted

Method

1 Add all the ingredients to the slow cooker and combine well. Cover and leave to cook for 2-3 hours making sure the granola doesn't burn. Serve with milk if you like.

CHEFS NOTE

This recipe is basically your favourite granola cereal combined with fresh fruit and spices to fill your kitchen with a lovely warming, welcoming aroma. Also good as a dessert with a little more sugar and a dob of fresh cream.

LOSE
WEIGHT
FOR GOOD
SLOW COOKER DIET
FOR BEGINNERS

SLOW COOKER SNACKS

BEAN, ROSEMARY & ROASTED GARLIC DIP

88 calories per serving

Ingredients

- 6 garlic cloves chopped
- 100g/3½ oz parmesan cheese grated
- 1 bunch chopped fresh rosemary
- 2 tbsp extra virgin olive oil
- 1 400g/14oz tin borlotti beans, drained
- 125g/4oz low fat cream cheese

- Handful chopped black olives
- 1 tbsp white wine vinegar
- 250ml/1 cup water
- 1 tbsp lemon juice
- Salt to taste

Method

1 Quickly pulse all the ingredients (except the lemon juice) in a food processor. Empty the blitzed mixture into the slow cooker and leave to cook on low for 1-2 hours. If the mixture is too thick, add a little more water. If it's not thick enough, continue to cook with the lid off until you get the required consistency.

2 After cooking allow to cool, stir in the lemon juice and serve with a selection of raw celery, cucumber and carrot batons.

CHEFS NOTE
This is a perfect low cal snack to keep you going between meals.

NACHO BEAN & ONION DIP

90 calories per serving

Ingredients

- 2 400g/14oz tins low fat refried beans
- 1 green chilli, finely chopped
- 1 onion, chopped
- 100g/3½ oz mozzarella cheese chopped
- 250ml/1 cup water
- Salt to taste
- 1 tbsp lemon juice
- 4 tsp taco seasoning mix

Or make your own:
- 2 tsp mild chilli powder, 1 ½ tsp ground cumin, ½ tsp paprika, ¼ tsp each of onion powder, garlic powder, dried oregano & crushed chilli flakes, 1 tsp each of sea salt & black pepper

Method

1 Place all the ingredients, except the lemon juice, into the slow cooker and combine well.

2 Leave to cook on low for 1-2 hours and before serving, stir in the lemon juice. If the mixture is too thick add a little more water. If it's not thick enough, continue to cook with the lid off until you get the required consistency.

3 Serve warm with plain tortilla chips.

CHEFS NOTE
Buffallo mozzarella is good in this recipe but regular mozzarella is fine too. Use the full fat versions of both.

HONEY ROASTED VEGETABLES

281 calories per serving

Ingredients

- 250g/9oz carrots
- 250g/9oz parsnips
- 1 tbsp balsamic vinegar
- 3 tsp runny honey
- 2 red onions
- 2 red (bell) peppers

- 2 tbsp olive oil
- 1 tsp each ground cumin, paprika, & chilli powder
- ½ tsp ground cinnamon
- 200g/7oz tinned chopped tomatoes
- Salt & pepper to taste

Method

1 Peel and cut the carrots, parsnips, peppers and onions into chunks.

2 Combine all the ingredients well in the slow cooker. Season, cover and leave to cook on low for 3-4 hours or until the vegetables are tender. Add a little water during cooking if needed.

CHEFS NOTE

This is a great Moroccan inspired dish which is also nice with some chopped apricots if you like additional sweetness.